Fourth of July Fireworks

by Patrick Merrick

Published by The Child's World®
1980 Lookout Drive
Mankato, MN 56003-1705
800-599-READ
www.childsworld.com

ACKNOWLEDGMENTS
The Child's World®: Mary Berendes, Publishing Director

The Design Lab: Kathleen Petelinsek, Design

Editorial Directions, Inc.: E. Russell Primm, Editorial Director; Joshua Gregory, Editorial Assistant;
Jennifer Zeiger, Fact Checker; Lucia Raatma, Copyeditor and Proofreader

PHOTO CREDITS
Cover and page 1, ©iStockphoto.com; page 5, ©ELEN, used under license from Shutterstock, Inc.; page 7,
©Monkey Business Images, used under license from Shutterstock, Inc.; page 9, ©iStockphoto.com/andi-
pantz ; page 11, ©iStockphoto.com/busypix; page 13, ©Daniel Hebert, used under license from Shutterstock, Inc.; page 15, ©littlesam, used under license from Shutterstock, Inc.; page 17, ©Alyona Burchette,
used under license from Shutterstock, Inc.; page 19, ©iStockphoto.com/efesan; page 21, ©sonya etchison,
used under license from Shutterstock, Inc.

LIBRARY OF CONGRESS CATALOGING-IN-PUBLICATION DATA
Merrick, Patrick.
 Fourth of July fireworks / by Patrick Merrick.
    p. cm. — (Our holiday symbols)
 Includes bibliographical references and index.
 ISBN 978-1-60253-334-9 (library bound : alk. paper)
1. Fourth of July—Juvenile literature. 2. Fireworks—Juvenile literature. I. Title. II. Series.
 E286.A1395 2010
 394.2634—dc22   2009035310

Printed in the United States of America
Mankato, Minnesota
November 2009
F11460

Table of Contents

Let's Watch the Fireworks!

The crowd grows quiet as it gets dark outside. It has been a very fun day. The best part is just about to begin, though. All at once, the sky is filled with colored shapes of light.

This is **Independence** Day. Those colorful flashes are fireworks!

A fireworks show is the perfect end to a fun celebration. Some shows can go on for over an hour!

What Is Independence Day?

Independence Day is a **holiday**. People celebrate it with their friends and families. It is a day for Americans to remember how their country got started.

Independence Day comes every year on July 4. Many people simply call it the Fourth of July.

Many people like to have cookouts to celebrate Independence Day. They gather with friends and family and eat delicious foods.

How Was This Country Started?

People began coming to America from England about 400 years ago. These **colonists** were still ruled by the King of England. They did not think he was a good king. After a while, the colonists decided to start their own country.

Americans fought for freedom in the **Revolutionary War**. This war lasted from 1775 to 1783. The colonists' military was not as strong as England's. They were still able to win the war, though.

During the war, the colonial leaders created the **Declaration of Independence**. It was accepted on July 4, 1776. The United States of America was born!

IN CONGRESS, JULY

The unanimous Declaration of the thirteen united States of

The Declaration of Independence turned the United States into its own country. It was no longer a part of England.

Do Many People Celebrate Independence Day?

Many people have different Independence Day **traditions**. Some people watch parades or play games with their families. Others remember the brave men and women who fought to keep the country free. For many people, the most exciting part of Independence Day is watching fireworks!

Independence Day is a great time to celebrate with family. Watching fireworks is even more fun when you do it with other people!

JUL
4

Why Do We Have Fireworks on Independence Day?

Fireworks have been around for almost a thousand years. Long ago, Chinese people used fireworks in many celebrations. This tradition was passed down and spread to other countries. American colonists used fireworks to celebrate the end of the Revolutionary War.

The Chinese invented fireworks a very long time ago. Chinese fireworks are sometimes decorated with traditional designs.

Where Are Fireworks Made?

The craft of making and setting off fireworks is called **pyrotechnics** (py-roh-TEK-niks). This is a very dangerous job. It is still done mostly by hand. There are fireworks companies in China, Europe, and the United States.

Fireworks shows are put on by people with special pyrotechnics training. This helps keep people from hurting themselves.

What Are Fireworks?

Fireworks are made from **gunpowder** and fire. Gunpowder wrapped in heavy paper burns so fast that it shoots into the sky and explodes! Fireworks makers also put special **chemicals** into the fireworks. This is what gives them their colors!

Firecrackers are types of fireworks that make loud popping noises. They do not shoot into the air or have colored explosions.

How Can We Use Fireworks Safely?

Fireworks are beautiful and exciting. They are also very dangerous! Fireworks injure many people every year. We must be very careful when we use them. We can all enjoy fireworks on Independence Day, as long as we make sure to stay safe.

Always remember to follow safety instructions when using fireworks. Even tiny sparklers can be dangerous.

Glossary

chemicals (KEM-ih-kuhlz) Chemicals are substances used in scientific processes.

colonists (KOL-uh-nists) Colonists were people who came from England and other parts of Europe to live in America.

Declaration of Independence (dek-luh-RAY-shuhn UHF in-di-PEN-duhnss) The Declaration of Independence is the document that first stated that the United States of America was a free country.

document (DOK-yuh-muhnt) A document is a written record of something.

gunpowder (GUHN-pow-dur) Gunpowder is a powder that explodes easily. Gunpowder is used to make fireworks.

holiday (HOL-uh-day) A holiday is a special day that people celebrate every year. The Fourth of July is a holiday.

independence (IN-duh-PEN-duhns) Independence is another word for freedom. The American colonists fought for independence from England.

pyrotechnics (py-roh-TEK-niks) Pyrotechnics is the craft of making and using fireworks.

Revolutionary War (rev-uh-LOO-shuh-nayr-ree WOR) The Revolutionary War was the battle between England and the colonies to make the United States a free country.

traditions (truh-DISH-uhnz) Traditions are ways of doing things that are passed down from generation to generation. Setting off fireworks on the Fourth of July is an American tradition.

Books and Web Sites

BOOKS

Heiligman, Deborah. *Celebrate Independence Day with Parades, Picnics, and Fireworks*. Washington, DC: National Geographic Children's Books, 2007.

Osborne, Mary Pope. *Happy Birthday, America*. Brookfield, CT: Roaring Brook Press, 2003.

Trueit, Trudi Strain. *Independence Day*. New York: Children's Press, 2007.

WEB SITES

Visit our Web site for lots of links about fireworks: *childsworld.com/links*

Note to Parents, Teachers, and Librarians: We routinely verify our Web links to make sure they are safe, active sites—so encourage your readers to check them out!

Index

About the Author

Patrick Merrick was born in California and spent much of his early life moving from town to town and from state to state. Eventually, his family settled in Sioux Falls, South Dakota. In addition to writing more than 45 children's books, Patrick has been teaching science to children for more than a decade. Patrick lives in southern Minnesota with his wife and five children. When not busy with school, writing, or parenting, Patrick enjoys the occasional nap.